It Is Hard to Look at

What We Came to Think

We'd Come to See

PITT POETRY SERIES
Ed Ochester, Editor

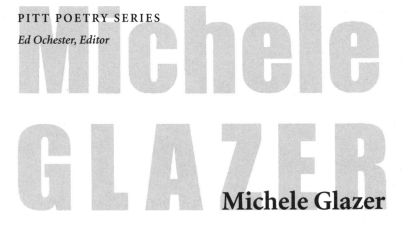

Michele Glazer

It Is Hard to Look at

What We Came to Think

We'd Come to See

UNIVERSITY OF PITTSBURGH PRESS

This book is the winner of the 1996 Associated Writing Programs' award series in poetry. Associated Writing Programs, a national organization serving over 150 colleges and universities, has its headquarters at George Mason University, Tallwood House, Mail Stop 1E3, Fairfax, Va. 22030.

Published by the University of Pittsburgh Press, Pittsburgh, Pa. 15261
Manufactured in the United States of America
Printed on acid-free paper
10 9 8 7 6 5 4 3 2

Library of Congress Cataloging-in-Publication data and acknowledgments are located at the end of this book.

A CIP catalog record for this book is available from the British Library.

The publication of this book is supported by a grant from the Pennsylvania Council on the Arts.

For my mother, Jean
For my father, Howard

in memory—
Shirley Blum Tanzer
John Cebern Pickett

Contents

Part 3

It Is Hard to Look at

What We Came to Think

We'd Come to See

Tourist

I. The Burning

River, and there is no water in it. There is the channel rushing
water made, one bridge, two shores. Before I see what's burning I see the burning.
Something turning
unfamiliar. I was walking to the river
to cross it. The river as the thing to cross.
And in the river,
nothing rushing nothing taking nowhere gone.
And that
was the river, I walk closer.

Wood stacked crosswise in the tsk tsk of cross purposes.
Burning straw is brought to light it, the straw tucked around the body catches,
    passes it
like relay runners their fierce baton.
And I know it's real because I happen on it. I am incidental,
happening on.
            On my shore
a man is circling the body, keening, running the erratic
planet of him and then the ever
narrowing circumference of his grief.
Wood smolders and smoke gathers
in the lungs of those who've come to mourn.

Fire burns the body into clarity.
The head throws off its caul, someone has taken
leave of itself, two bright feet.
There are two sides to everything.
Then again there is the river.
And the others sit apart, casually because it wants to be
a celebration. Someone is turning orange and yellow.

But the one who is circling, he is
thickening around their necks, he is the neck,
he is the blazing necklace of grief.

II. The Circus

Still, it's the same, the likely and the unlikely,
whether she can hold the quivering hole her rope draws in
the air—   she does not care.
If I thought I came to see them balance
I stayed to see if they would fall,
where the show failed, where it would show itself as show.
Couples juggle first plates then chairs then flaming candles.
I reaffirm the pattern by looking for the error,

                            the gesture uncompleted,

                                            the *amiss.*

Two bodies balanced head to head trade impossible postures
for applause. Their faces insist it hurts.
What do *I* know? The ground under my feet?
My chair is hard.
The girl whose swirling rope will not spin wide enough for her to enter
the turning circle of it lets drop the whole,
gives back one burning look and goes.
The lights are bright but not right here.
I sit up close.
I visit the bottoms of the aerialist's feet.

Part 1

Morning Glory

Morning glory tangles a simple landscape
of fence and poles, assuming the shape
of what it grips. Whatever it grips,
grips it; scribbles a vine fence, vine porch.

Morning glory wraps around a pole like a heart
around a little finger.
The leaves are shaped like dark trite hearts.
If I tear it out it is still
beyond anything I can name.

The blossoms are pentagonal white.

White arms, two fat legs.
Head, no fat curls. Bald. Baby bald.

He comes awake one morning into the world.

The blooms   open   like radiant caves

His eyes have not found their color.
His is a mouth wholly dependent.
What I whisper in his ear keeps him
from hearing: You will never be more yourself.
Love holds him.
Soon words will fill him.
He will want to please.

The blooms nod

I would almost warn him
but if he heard, already

it would be too late.
Taking the shape of other people
he will assume his name.

A baby comes awake. Listen
to the rush of morning
glory, to each bloom
clean as a new tooth.

Fruit Flies to the Too Ripe Fruit

Fruit flies are useful in studies of heredity
because they multiply readily and are easy to keep.

From a bowl, deeply between green apples some things stir

like inklings of a long secret.

When the boy asks *where do they come from,* say *never.*

Not to exist until the fruit rots and then be

ubiquitous is the secret to a long memory.

Some are drawn to the spoiling.

Some sweat out of the smooth-skinned fruit

the way buried in a question is another question.

When the boy asks *how do you know*

toss out the hollowed cantaloupe to loosen the flies.

When the boy asks *where do they disappear to* whisper

always

Not to exist long but to metamorphose with each
individual extinction is the secret to a long shadow.

In this version of the story the father moves out.

Boar Baroque

Under the awning *charcuterie,*
      among market stalls surging
with watercress, red potatoes, garlic ropes the boar hangs.
Nothing's distended.
It is a pendulum,
      a compass,
            the needle pointing south; I hang back wondering
why no flies gather,
no one stares.

Noon, and the food's left to perch till 3.
A landscape of chives and endive,
         the vaguely ornamental around
     the pure dead thing.
What floats inside each hedge of incremental eyelashes?
         The left is dense,
    or rather, potent,
the other's slightly mottled
    as if someone stuck
a stick into its color and stirred
    in a little yellow.
         Two together
have that glossy look of one
    who having thought himself beloved
is disinherited.
In its approximation to perfection,
     the boar's obscene.

    Accustomed to pheasants clutching air,
things skinned and neatly dismembered—the boar confuses me.
Is it a thing?
    Even more,

they confuse me, who move around it
　　　　　　　like an ordinary tragedy.
Each day I visit hoping to see it
　　　　　　somehow used, a simple subtraction, a shoulder
gone as if the difference
　　　　　　　between animal and meat is what's hacked out.
I like a surface
　　　　　　marred, the damage
　　　　and the cause, the underneath
of things, where sight fails,
　　　　　the way certain music slows
　　　　　　and stops
　　　　　　　　　　　　and catches.
　　　　　　The bristly piñata turns, the forgiving
　　　　　　　　wall it hangs against gives up
　　　its secret,
　　　　　　　　　the dark crimson wink joining anus to throat, that
long
　　　　　slit where well-being slipped out. And I
imagine something softening,
　　　　　　　decay　　　　　taking its time,
that taking back, the taking in by
organisms too
　　　　　　small to summarize,
appetite feeding
　　　on the whole idea.

All That in the Voice I Have Adopted for This Lie*

(for J. K.)

Fresh figs blacken and sweeten.
The Mediterranean sun lengthens and roots,
tipped by a nimble surer than a dowser's wand, sink
like the dream into the dreamer.
On top a woman walks about.
To wend the invisible is to know
the obstacle before they meet.
She knows these leaves
are fleshy with an inference
she restrains herself from touching and feels lush
in her restraint.
Too-sweet, the figs
rot.

    She's had enough, she knows what they are doing,
roots waking to receding water.
Naked, in the shower, and her feet, naked too, of course, she stands
inches deep in the brackish back-up, the color swirling   —no
no-color —   it's the shadow
cast by water,
an appalling and miraculous
root-soup.

    They are waking and she knows it.
There is no wobble down there.
All direction is toward desire
if desire's felt. How often she is
two ways at once.
She is old and bends
easily. She is thin.
She is on her knees, with both hands
she wends the snake down in.

*The title is a line from the poem "Winter: The Problem With Music" by Robin Reagler.

Science

Larkspur——bluemoss——his deciduous hands——
oh, but why would you want to?
He is somber honey.
He is a mouthful of bees.

In the Cleaning Room

—at the natural history museum

Rhetorical to ask
if a muscle's flex
is felt by an exact
description
of the knee's geniculation

to accommodate its faith?
Relax, you have begun
inspection of the wreck.
Watch, now, grubs riot
the flesh like the intimate

corruption when emotion
stubborns itself. But
no, separate, though their hunger conforms
precisely
to the cartilage; they are effacing

the flesh, describing
incessantly as tongues.
The skull with-
draws as it's
revealed: stoic.

Then in the tank, in the glass tank, some-
thing shifts; the unfleshed
defies hunger; she does not know, then, has the skull become
itself, nearly,
or is it almost vacant, about to be

constructed? The specimen
will stay until it's——

The woman leaves and shuts
the door.
As a freshly falling. As a fresh leaf falling, she's quiet.

And what she can she won't.

Real Life #2: Scraps

Althea kept a list of the things she could live without—perfumed soaps, clean rugs, cats. It was a long list. She added to it from scraps she wrote on when she thought of them. Every fortnight or so she gathered up the scraps and in her ancient and exquisite longhand added them to her bound list. Love wasn't on it but a list of the people she might have expected it from was. Who did he think she was? The shiny sleeve he wiped his mouth on? *Sit down* her husband said on the telephone one afternoon after she got home. The possibility of slow transformation strains the modern sensibility but change occurs, the reef's meticulous accrual, the iceberg melts and floods ensue. Even a rise of one degree in temperature and slowly, slowly. People rise in trees. *Sit down. I have something to tell you.* So then he said, *I've got something good to tell you.* Out the window the sky is flat as an old cheek. There is no end to it. Althea takes out a clean page and draws a line down the middle. Column A, she titles *The Ones I Love;* Column B is *The Ones Who Love Me.* The sky is flat and she can touch it.

She blushes. Not the fine weather of inevitability. Not desire, that fringed purse, but she feels just fine. What's left? And does she bless the pressed flowers of occasion? Outside,

the sky. *"My visibility is greatly enhanced,"* she writes, *"by the flatness of the terrain."*

Jungle Crabs Near Nicaragua

Each part brightly articulated
As if it belongs to itself first
And then the crab.
And there are sounds of something out
Of place. Claws chatter the street.
Giddy, we tense
Before each body's thickness, anticipate
Cracking the flesh, then squat to watch, answering
Their grasps with a lunge.

Only for cars do we make ourselves visible;
A single light gives some driver the choice
To swerve.
We talk loud nonsense, flaunting ourselves
Harmless, while the living drag the crushed off to eat
Or keep them.

They are yours, I think. You carry them with you
Any way you can.
They are yours. We are the foreign language
In a night of moving parts.

Part 2

Her Eyes

He kisses her but only with his lips.
His eyes digress — skid — dart — deflect,
Waterstriders on a summer lake
Moving by the grace of being
Moved by something
Smaller than themselves.
Or larger: hunger.
(What is he looking at?)
Does lake hang from the tips of their stubborn snappable legs? But the fine
Surface halos where, after all, the legs dip, touching it, not
Entering. He kisses her, love looks
Like this: A man
Inside himself
Fiercely, where the kiss
Originates.

Ode to the Room of the Dead Fish
& to the Dead Fish

Anything that goes wrong goes here, in a jar.
Here are the soft fish,
digressive.
The flesh
misspelling itself.
They suffer the glass like a wish
I press my face
hard against,
squinting into the light.
What wanting shapes them?
The four-eyed, the fin-holed, all sort
of tumor, all white, almost
opaque, a circus
of bad births.
In Bangkok the faithful press
gold scales onto available buddhas.
Where it's hardest to see
brings the most luck.
Everything's strange enough.

I enter the room where the moons dwell.
I've been here before,
to the tongue's slur,
the blurted out no-cause
I-love-you's.
They are like each bad time with a loved one
one holds for how
it eases the inevitable loss and for this
we love the fish.
From so many seas they are their own
democracy.
O arabesque fish!

Whey-faced congestive
genetics.

Now you hold
the best seats in the house,
all glass frontages.

There is no door to the room of the dead fish.
The room glows.
There are no odes. Nodes. No, they are owed
us who make a museum
of them.

Still the room glows.
I will forget the fish. . . .
When I forget the fish
what will be there to remember
the whiteness by?
Everything's strange enough.
You don't have to make up anybody.
You don't have to miss anything.
You don't have to speak
above a modest prayer, but if you do. If you ask.
If you're wrong . . . as if
one misconception
dissipates
the weight of our necessary fear.

Seizing the Storm

These are the One-and-a-Halfs, full humans with
incomplete 'parasitic' bodies attached to their own.

Confronting them, I could feel the final horror
evoked by the Freaks stir to life: a kind of vertigo like
that experienced by Narcissus when he beheld his image
in the reflecting waters and plunged to his death.

Freaks, Leslie Fiedler

I.

    The Half's head (assumed)
is bedded in the belly of its living brother.
    Buttocks, legs and back extend
as clear parts
      of an unclear plan. In this
it is like history: indiscrete.

Or rather, like history before
    its end was audible.
No instructions come with it.
What name do you give your brother?

Your brother makes you a   uh.
But there are whole days, who doesn't want to come out of nowhere
    A visible orphan   A new race
      Not repeating anyone's mistakes.

I envy that the evil done you
    those years of looking
back at those who looked, to whom
    you were a Look,
was personal. An accident
   of birth, but of <u>your</u> birth.

An 11th finger is nothing I can point to—
  I cannot point to anything
about History about Destiny.
  What name

do you give your brother? You proved the world
  resists our will
to divide against
  its nature. Resisted in your pure
embodiment of blur——
  <u>*monster*</u>.

II.

Now the storms are "Gloria" and "Eleanor."

III.

<u>You</u> <u>got</u> <u>that</u> <u>right</u>, Friend
says eyeing the woman applying
layers of pink oil crayon
to the faintly described mouth, revising, accentuating
lines she keeps
safe inside of.
Waxy pupils hug an inner and an outer canthus.
Bad news makes her grip
the color stick, digging into the paper the color
and the color's shape.
A mirror is propped. (Her easel's
propped.) In the middle she's the one
trying to draw her way out.
She leaves out all background, though
the lawn is wide, the pines knurled
enough to seem more than an incidental

gesture to the public street. <u>Yes</u>,
it's <u>awful</u>, and smudges the eyes
just so (<u>a</u> <u>face</u> <u>this</u> <u>exact</u>), eases
the anger out of the hot rose madder mouth, so,
relentlessly slurring the grimace
into something softer, kinder,
more pleasing that she loses—

                        shortly—

the graphic hope on the real
face. *What name do I——*
Does the hair last, marking it in rapidly in caesius waves.

Jungle

Do you doubt my—

                   do you?

I pretend to see what you see.

I pretend to see what you pretend.

I see, I do, what you pretend to, *don't* you?

Don't *I?*

Who, now, would rather *die* first for the other?

Why should I fear the lie

The white lie burning simple and clear

Enough that we can make it anything we call it?

We call it **love**. We believe anything.

Don't interrupt, please, is there—

What monarch butterflies eat is poison to what eats them.

                                    —Another solution?

Here's the story, then, of the "Boy (Eaten by Bears)." The fabled
brows of bears kept us serious once-upon. Outside the bear is
the bear. Inside the bear is the subcutaneous layer, for which **bear**
is another name, and the fat is **bear** and the blood shocked red
by exposure. And the parts that are themselves are **bear** and it's
bear to the bone. But the skeleton of a large bear looks almost
exactly like the skeleton of a man and you can't be certain
if you have the man wrong. I think this is one of the stories
we're left. By which we're left.

Real Life #7: Summer

Mabel Jones is hanging his Depends up on a line in the kitchen. He's 98
and she's his daughter. When she'd thought about it she thought she'd die
a fat old lady. All her life she'd been kind of cowed by him, now since the illness
he's grown skinny. All summer she opens cupboards, hauls out unopened
boxes of cereal and opens them to reveal their clumsy contents,
moths and larvae in packages of cookies, flour, Grape-Nuts.
Each moth stunned, wrapped in its own wings like a person wakened
into speech by a phone ringing. After a winter warm enough that they bear up,
they bear. Were they born in there? Come wrapped in waxed paper?
Mabel Jones tosses everything that shows a sign, some shape amiss among
the small brown contents. A webbiness to the rice. Pearly maggots,
thick and short and vastly segmented, inch fast up the horseteeth-white walls,
along the ceiling. There is a sort of caged-in smell of rank urine in the kitchen,
if he could smell it. *They'd fall apart if she washed them, who can afford it?*
Her right knee hurts again and she applies some pressure. And she knows
that everything she smells she smells because it enters her. It attaches.
It's molecules and atoms and it comes up her nose, her _olfactories_. Think of that
when the hallway stinks after your father, bless him, flushes.

                                                 A chaos of residential moths
into her face. Moths winging the air like stupored flies, moths ganging up
like soft memories. *No, flies don't flutter.* What is this movement of wings that gives
flutter to one, purpose to the other? Purpose she understood as intelligence
or motive. What is the temperature of change, how will she know it?
Two moths mating look like one large moth until, swatted, they fall, they fall apart,
fall into one ecstatic death. Think of the diesel smell of buses and of the things
you think that you can walk away from. Think of how you take it all with you,
in you. And how it starts, maybe, a little spot of cancer. *But he was good to her.*
She didn't wash them. You can imagine the smell. Of course he can't smell a thing.

How old he is! The larvae are livelier than him, and faster. But the moths, their inept and unrehearsed flutterings! One takes up where another leaves off. She presses one into the wall. Now there is a stirring, now there is a faint mark.

Star-Spangled

One man won't say anything.

One says over to himself
  oh say can you see

anything

The world rolls under his tongue
as a muddy river enjoins the bank

join me. Or
    watch me

    roll on.

Fourteen years later and he's still fresh home from Nam.

If he could just tell his story he'd get

A better job. More money. His health back.
If he had time

doing it would be as easy as two sticks.

Afraid of missing
                something

he leans forward—
      What is the difference between a subject
      and a noun Why do we need both Do

rhetorical questions get question
marks Why
            do we need both

How does it feel to be back

I want to ask him and

How does it feel to be you

His secret is he knows
he doesn't belong here.

One night I bring a cut-out, white
on black or black

on white, is the question.
Is it a vase or two faces seen

in profile and from a long distance?
Did "the tailback who injured his knee recently

return to practice"?
Or did he recently return?

That night the weather turns.
All night everything will happen

under one color.
In the middle of class he gets up,

walks out into it.
"Apostrophes show possession,"

says one woman after he leaves.
"But if you just say it

you don't need them."
One night in the middle of his question

he stops. His words
turn back to him suddenly, a black

funneling of swifts down a chimney.
It is a mystery why

they choose one chimney over another
and how so many birds fit inside.

And Sand Dollars

I.

What's broken wasn't bought in a gift shoppe.
I stub against them, half-buried and hope—
Though broken is authentic,
I keep the most complete because completion is vulnerable.
As in   What good luck we had we know because it broke.

Not like the ocean breaking on the whole shore,
not *striking* equally, but *striking* everywhere.
Here and there, spent between lengths of unremarkable beach,
vacancies bloom around extinct lives.

If one can recreate the beast from a single tooth,
how is the body behind an utterance?
What is it the body asks?

II.

What rises in the morning out my window is a goose
tethered for its broken beak to heal. Some consonant hissing.
Some goose hiccuping shredded lettuce from a white bucket.
It twists the cord around one orange leg.
It is frantic to be freed.
It is frantic when I try to free it. It is

Night, still. What is it solid to vision the body moves through?
Up the cliff some people fill their window with light.
It makes the darkness they look into deeper. It makes them
the one seen thing imagining, perhaps,
perhaps a seer,
themselves some gift.

Dowsers' Convention, McIver State Park

The day's remains already packed in Styrofoam.
Can the meeting be dismantling? I've only come.
But no,
A few chairs still overflow with over-
Alls and muted calicos.
Look, I want the man whose few lank hairs belie
His scalp to know I know, I want that
Ruddy belle to know I know.
There is dust at my knees. Dust quilting my tongue.
They have the sticks they have the faith.
How easily I can think them into slow
Cows facing the same way home where dinner
Ends finally in slaughter.
What did I miss?
Who is in charge here?
This man old enough to look authentic holds
An ample wishbone.
For each foot deep he paces one direction.
Why does nothing move me?
But when his wrists confirm
The water the gases or what-
Ever he's after, doubt lifts
Me.
What possible attraction of water
To divining rod?
What moves him is the know-
Ledge of another's belief.
(These currents made visible with wishes that are weeds.)
Wind ticks through the Scot's broom.
He holds his rod like a stinky shoe he has been sent
To fetch.
Or a beloved dead pet.

This is business.
I'll plant weeds.
And yet, how green it is, as if only green
And blue are reproducing.
And I am fossil-logical, without a clue.
What in his world permits him meaning
Where he looks, certain
Anything inside the earth moves with him?
But when god's presumed to be
Guiding his divining rod, I have to leave and walk uphill
Until I've got my pockets full of broken-
Open pods of Scot's broom.
The line is moving.
They'll be following their headlights home all night.

I'm afraid it shows.
Nothing moves me.

Where is the other, *real* show?

These seed pods grind and crack, small boats in a violent mooring.

Or is it the music
Of vessels calmly ditched by whatever

    Intelligence once haunted them

Not This,

      but that
Cell-on-cell-particular assembles
Grass.
      Are we beside ourselves?
How botanists explain the sanguinary leaves
      Of fall: Long nights. The cold.
The way we must say *damn*
To get the tent down.
The same way we got the tent up.

Without Title

When my father on the phone to his stockbroker breaks

Into tears, it's his tumor talking.

And what he can not say, cannot

Remember, that

Is tumor, too.

But what he did not say was the

Part that spread;

Became the largest part of him;

Became him, as snow flatters

What it covers

Becomes it, becomes

The spreading part.

Its own.

Pomegranate

In how she slits the thin matte cheek without popping even a single
blister lies the character of the woman. How fortunate she is
to have a sharp knife, though that is not chance. Unlike banana rind
the skin resists one direction. Its remonstrant *thwack* is of something
clearly broken, something damaged. The woman might have cut a deep
rift into the fruit and had only pulp and flesh protest. But damage
is necessary. Have two pomegranates ever broken open to the same
design? Nor does she receive each seed individually Nor are they
thumbed out in palmfuls Nor do her lips prod the sphagnum flesh.
The flesh retains its signature of seed long after she knocks the pulp
into a hobbled wine glass. Now a section of the fruit has been emptied.
Now she lifts the glass,

swelling her cheeks with seed, risking the joke that expels each to its
small red meaning. It has no flavor at all. There are stories, too,
of the various ways men eat corn, the movement of their lips, the way
the ear travels habitually. A few are said to hold it perpendicular
to the earth. What is revealed about such men? (Where are their noses?)
They must be watchful. The movement of her lips is guileless, mellifluous,
lush as a grass skirt. Is she a song, yellow and full of flower?
Say around a thing or it will elude you. To know the fruit, the seed,
praise what it exposes.

Pueblo

The ones we can't visit are the reason we come.
The ones we can visit are the ones we pass.
Past saleable turquoise and silver, stopping for drums
On the way, thumping
The sun-bleached cowhide
Taut over truncated aspen, tree I know by its eyes that trace clear
Through its heart.

       If I scraped the heart out the eyes
Would stay. I'm tired
Of miles of, not talk, but
That the topical is all scenery—
Chit-chat-chit-chat-chit of a clock ticking.
From the sides of the road we drive I feel them look.
How *they* look.
How they *look* and then they turn away to walk.
How the pueblo gave up what it was to become how *it* looked: a failed four-level
Defense that long ago raised from the dust its moral eyebrows
Four levels. It's four dollars to park here,
Two more to take photos. Where is the sound
Of the language that, because I can't understand each word, means more?
We understand each other's words. We don't   <u>Let's</u> <u>not</u>
<u>Talk</u> <u>about</u>   We   <u>Look</u> <u>at</u> <u>that</u> <u>sculptural</u> <u>rock</u> <u>that</u> <u>rock</u>   <u>that</u>

       Dust stirs up stirs
Our departure. We leave their stream-whose-origin-is-forbidden, the comeupon
Tumulose plot of wooden crosses knotted
With weeds and fenced off, no one's been buried here in years.
Too soon it will be late, too
After, too never after. On the road
Out the land recedes into a visit.

On the road home which is any road out
New steel ribs are being slapped over with adobe,
Like a petticoat giving the dress body, giving
The body its whisper stiff life,
The one we can't visit
That we live.

Detritus

It is the same only more so.
No one is home, or

Whoever came came
Too late; it is still.

Still, someone comes
And someone stays to see

What's coming.
A lack of color is not black.

It's the intestinal pale of sea rope,
Of worms born in to matter reeling

And deeply blind. Of what has never lived
Outside the body.

Inside.
From where I am it's all

The same. It is
More so is lethal. Behold

The differences? My words are
Happy to be orphans. Be-

Hold what difference
Any-of-it makes.

At the shore the appetite of flies over any rotting matter.
I wish I could

It Is Hard to Look at What We Came to Think We'd Come to See

Everybody knew what you were going to do before you did it.

You couldn't go out without encountering
Some version of yourself, oh, years old
You thought you had let go of,
Like that narrow hall, the row of frames
Contiguous along the wall, you walk down,

walk down.

> *Look, here are crows the way a child draws them, urgent m's*
> *their wings extended*
> *and the earth's a gorgeous proof*
> *of insanity, that bright kinetic wheat.*
> korenveld met kraaien. *You wanted those hard K's,*
> *the sky's*
> *blue fingerprints you could almost identify*
> *as if what Van Gogh saw and what he saw with*
> *made the same terrible strokes.*
> *These crows have no eyes, no need and if they had*
> *would close, close up.*

The frames are down
And sunlight nails onto the wall
Explicit shapes "... **as simply shape.** ...
Liberated windows, no view into,

out of.

Of Da Vinci's cartoon, the expert said,
"If I had a painting this torn I'd trash it."

He can't restore
            the picture the man
      mad at
who knows what
            shot holes in.
Later you were still there
. . . not as description,

                              not as reminiscence," the way sudden
Birds aren't birds but the configuration
Fear wakens.

He can't make the picture whole again.
He makes damage the thing we look for
            because it's there. . . .
                        look now
what breaks. . . . it is like this
            everywhere
                        . . . becomes
the reason
            we come to look.

Variations on a Fixed Target

He can block out with two fingers moving
held before his eyes above the one flat
stand of fir below the ridge the shape
of what he got up early, this morning,
and came down here to the river,
hoping to recognize.

Or he can not look up.

Now there are five of them.
　　Retina tugging on the vitreous humor
sets off free-floating flakes of an eye
lost in their own element.

　　Bald eagles travel another way; though
floaters have a reason, it isn't theirs.

Theirs is a small thing idling; any fish
lolling near the river's nervous
surface draws them low over the ridge.
And what the man can't see *(what*
is he lost in?): them,
plummeting for rodents
on the river-soaked island.

Into a likewise forest you walked, once.
Out of a plastic bag you drew
the fist they made, examined it, then
loosened your father's ashes.
　　　　　　　Released, you said,

until there was no telling
what parts of his body
     rose,
          what parts caught in the rocks.
And you hold those ashes
in your mind, feathers of a bird you miss
you want to know the habits of.

You refuse to know the habits of.

How close the porous flakes
you would not name *(not my*
father, *anymore)* fell.
How far?

Once, in a field.
Webs, stitching shut the tall grasses,
shiny secrets the sunlight told
then recanted.
A mist of spiders cast adrift, *ballooning*—
(our bodies were a blind itch)
—whatever stopped them was home.
(I have read there are passages
through a body, Tom,
a bullet can pass touching nothing vital.)
Is that survival,
wanting to be snagged that way,
drawn up into the migrating
blues and greens
into the fugitive light and *I don't*
want to know . . . you turn; turn
your face up into everything
blue moving.
And everything else lets it.

corkscrew: a short history of a short Relationship

*Nothing spoils the act of a man trying / to play host like a
corkscrew / that disembowels the cork and drops / the
shattered remains / into the bottle.*

Unknown

I.

He says You have to tie down
everything I say He says
I'm getting up now.
I'm walking out that window.
I've heard *that* before
(I think), a chained dog
prowling its yard. Forgetting its chain
when it smells its purpose: You Keep Out

II.

Moist in the mouth in the storm.

III.

The roses are a dollar each Do you want me
He says to buy

IV.

you one?

V.

Here is my heart laid He
says out like Kansas
under your summer
(What do you *think* [He says]

VI.

I mean?) Wheat.

VII.

There is one thing wrong here.
And one green thing.

VIII.

In the storm where are we safe?

IX.

There are the ones you love and.

X.

There are the ones who love you.

XI.

His stroking my hand that salt lick

and the deer's tongue mild
over it.

XII.

Try to remember now He says
What is the last thing you remember?
Write it down here.
Is that all.
Do you remember how I'll

XIII.

keep it for you.

You

I.

Some fever. Memories singed sweetdeep
that she must   upstream
to them to overwhelm them, drown them, plunge them
down under with the bitter ones.
With why it never would have worked.
She holds them
down the way once she had held his head
between her legs.

II.

Something curls up into just about nothing.
All matter is preserved.
You doused the hot coals with fuel, lit it.
We were smoke unfurled, we were
impossible.
The delirium of sword-
ferns into coal;
as close down as the coal burns itself,
that's how.

"The Purpose of Design Is to Make the Whole Greater Than the Sum of Its Parts"

1)
That red-shafted flicker in the woods.
        Is it the one you claimed
Probed the one oak? Can you hear it?

        Decay has its own
Small life; the bird heard
        It and, entering, turned it

        From abstraction into flesh.

1)
If long ago we made things longer
        By piecing the parts together, then
Whole years passed this way
        And that.

1)
What is *in*
        To a hole any flicker might
Slip through?

1)
The oak died and the bird didn't kill it.

1)
One hole nearly fills this scab
        Of bark. And the hole

Insists, doesn't it,
     On a *here* and a *there*
Out of the air. Now your mouth

Wraps around a sound
     That will not let you out.

     If I could piece the parts . . . , part

With the pieces . . .

1)

               Lay down your head now don't you
     Feel almost at home?

1)

     One gnat to
Whom fine mesh may be
     Invisible will fill an eye.
What blunders.
     Your good blue eye it drowns
In, too large
     To see.

1)
And this isn't about
You, really. What
Is?

Part 3

Sequence, Costa Rica

I.

Green stutter on a mangrove root
blends to mangrove. We mix them up.
Cicadas blur the air. The air is dusk
like father half understood.
We make it up. We put our tongues out,
shaping the world with the prehensile
strength of our tongues. Still,
it is a blue nuzzle of a day.
Chameleon tongue flicks home a fly.
Chameleon to a fly is a flash of air, *eclipse*.
Chameleon looks at me at an angle from which
I cannot see myself.

II.

That a thing banal as dirty clothes nested a shudder.
It was no sign, its coconut hair, its thickness.
The horror, more than half, was in the word, *tarantula*
I would not touch.
Too thick to kill and, its awkward sac grotesque,
vulnerable, it might expel a quiver of eggs.
Stiff under a glass on newspaper. I shunted it to a window letting
all her beautiful obstacles become her parachute—become the saved.
I would rather believe in indifference
than in a god of anger or rejoicing;
in a green and rusty world with restraints sometimes opaque as paper,
sometimes lucent before the lovely alienness,
in which we cannot make, except these small, choices.

III.

I wanted edges sharp enough to hurt.
Angry veterans live here wanting (a)
Both (b) amnesia (c) paradise.
And so we live in the munificence of smugglers.
At dusk the world, the road looks mossy flat.
A flat world was safe for it had edges.
And were the people who died then the survivors?
Past a violently ragged umbrella pitched on an open gate
A man approaches whose face is out of context.
And the parts are interchangeable?
"When the gates are open the dogs are out to keep
Police and, you know, away.
A man from Colorado disappeared four days ago."
And you could stop yourself from falling, couldn't you?
". . . to lose your self" means
What? Of the umbrella, "The dogs did that.
The dogs

IV.

It could have been anything from a distance, a bluff
In my bright safe laundry. And then it was tarantula.
Was it the hirsute lie in the history
I was right to believe? Or truth in the glossy lie?
Either way, it took a long time to see.
Slowly I saw its sac of new life, its many good-byes.
It was out of my morning's habit even so,
An illicit fact I let go. But the fact was
Sleeping in its presence wasn't overcoming a fear.
It was —that's impossible— turning —was inevitable— a new leaf.
"Your father . . ." Mother began once after
Father walked out. It's what
                    You can't unknow
        some hysterical touch.

It's nature and it's death. It's
Easy. It's
". . . Oh. Of course . . ." and walk away——— a new life.

V.

From any one place to another, wanting to let in any.
Wanting to give over to the river under our sway-
Backed craft; under the cracked shell of our vessel
We stir, adrift to Tortuguero.
Out of their life-festering nests green turtles drag;
We float, leaving our wake like the abandoned
Sand-threading track of a tail to the sea.
       Through a grim crack in the rotted timber the blue
Ruptures. And how readily the mind breaks into
A not knowing not caring again one thing
From another.

VI.

All night out of the trees they drop, and from the sand
Skitter up the diagonal slick of tent flap, canvas
Sides; like a mind inside, we, blunted and fluxed by so many
Monkeys and crustaceans not yawing to get in but simply
On their way; we are in their way from any
One place to another, wanting to let in any — oh come back —   But
They, too, pass over our hunch in the green dimming
Swoop under the many leaves of canopy in the many, showing us no
Mind. We can not know a crab from the wind heaving rotten coconuts;
Even when our eyes work, on sides and roof—
It is all top and sides undifferentiated—we see
Only the impressions of feet as if we are buried and the walkers
On us pack dirt down.

Love Poem

The bigger of the two is moving.
It looks so soft she would like to run
her hand over it so she runs
her eyes over it.
She wills them closer. She will not look
at the identical houses she passes
walking home, wanting
to leave each the privacy.
Walking this far to dump the wilted flowers.
When she moves her arms
unleash odors.
The young one browses.
Being young it has less to be alert to.
She can almost touch it. Frightened
at the kindness. The kindness of deer bribed
out of their better instinct.

A Violence in Wings

I.

I listened for the shiny sound
    of coins and stopped watches
beneath the lawn and thought of it
            as rescue
because I heard
    their restful soughs
as a fierce clicking. I thought
    I was looking for treasure, tracing
as a chalk drawing around the body
            marks how
    the body fell. In dusk
          of dive-bombing swifts
I was looking for clues.

My presence was a violence in wings.
Their flight was a thought
    I could not follow,
        an assumption. For instance,
    the way evening grafts to afternoon.
What holds each
        separate is how
    it catches light. Light, that is,
    to see, to catch change
on the wing,
    on the cusp of wing where it's feather
        and light, I can follow.

II.

     In a small house, burying.
(the story having to start somewhere, digging the story up)
     In a small way two people alone
             (but where?)
in a hate, each needing the other
to be there
to hate back.
     Hiding
things. *(how*
do I know?) Forgetting
     what they hid. The hate
not hidden. *(but*
     where?) One day
     one died. The one left
lay for days on a rug flat
with dog hair and wood ash
watching marines invade her field of lupine.
Their solid bodies converged
paling into contours.
They vanished where they found her.
Madness, too, brought back the man—you, who widowed her.
Desire and revenge were her single mind.
     (having to know now,
                 getting the story "straight" . . .)
She had the hate right.

III.

     Light throws us visibly
apart; trees root
     between it; each bird assumes
its own flight, each wing.
Night makes us one. But lost.

Is there another name for where they meet?

If expectation is dread;
             if by looking
I transform the thing I seek,
     did I want to know
though I looked
       looking as if I wanted to?
In the pantry coffee cans haggard
the shelves with dimes and pennies
tucked behind tomato paste and Spam.
      You hid
your coins from her; she hid
     hers, in the same room
a shelf apart.

Real Life #4: Playground

Already the evening air is quick with children gathering up discarded jackets and preparing to drift alone or in twos and threes out of the park, children in airy huddles like dandelions in that fragile quivering silver moment when they have gone to seed but retain some semblance of their former shape, the shape of flower which the wind dismantles, leaving the ragged clumps to drift off, the night to absorb them. On the day the children's mother dies Alma is sitting them. The boy, now bent over under the swing, is brushing bark chips off his knees. Someone had to be there when the children woke up. Someone had to wake them, bathe them, tell them something.

This last-chance giddy exhaustion, the girl spinning herself dizzy on the merry-go-round, the boy pumping himself still higher in the swing — what is the sense of their leaving for home any sooner than they need to? She thinks of their old life. Already the tops of the trees have vanished. *What were we doing that day?* they will ask years from now. So why hurry? They will want to hear over and over the same story as if it contained clues to how some previous civilization lived. She will make them play all night until they beg with limp bodies for her to take them home to bed. They will remember this thing that is happening, their futures rearranging even as their faces dim, the players reshuffling even as the ground moves under the girl's spinning body, the boy's legs flying. They will remember the day *this* way, the way she shapes it for them. *She doesn't know how much longer she can keep them there, playing.* The abandoned slide gives off moonlight and home is close by.

My

Indifference is an art; it takes practice.
You holding to your kite string have learned
To show you are responsible
For what the wind does. What the wind does
I watch behind a window
You do not know. You fret
The cord, the weightlessness and drag are all yours.

Summer, & Her Painted Flowers

She is all definition, the woman, her summer
Dress pleated with sweat.

In the firm prow of her belly, in the hold
Her cargo settles
In, as if to stay.

When it comes she will be flat
Which is herself again,

Another.

Outside dry grasses nudge each other *as if
to say*

Lie still again, then.
(All of the angles make sense to the wind.)

Everything here is animal is quick
To touch and soft to bite.
The man will die.

All of the eyes in back of him are women's eyes.

For now, though, look
How tenderly she holds his head, magnificent, immense,
Tipped like a beggar's soft wool cap.

It's hard for him.
It takes both of them to hold it.

What a field her mouth makes

On his. All of the eyes. All of the ways
He's seen, women see.

Letting the Glue Dry

Every building is in scale Do you see
Can you picture them full size Can you believe
I keep thinking of my neighbor
who paid $100 extra to have his mother
turned regularly.
Still she had bedsores.
the patience this took to construct
How many years do you think it took to glue
the wood, counting the time letting the glue dry
Guess the number of nails Look
The bed didn't lie.
                              at their size
No, we are not Amish.
I don't know where the Amish live, exactly.

Don't you wonder how he thought of it
Look at the barn, see any nails There aren't any
Can you find the corn crib and granary,
The sores ran.
the Kinderschule Guess how many screws
in the granary Is this how you
thought Lincoln's village would look
What was the price per roof
It isn't that
they couldn't turn her fast enough.
No, you won't see any hanged witches here
It always happens, seeing her he has
too much to say to no one.
Where are you from?
There is nothing like this anywhere.

Which diorama do you like best
Do you know how he cut the beveled glass
for all those windows Do you think
    To make her whole again he would have
    made himself a child.
he sewed the curtains himself
No the Amanas are not a religious community
primarily We voted fifty years ago to join
the system of free enterprise
    River's a queer place to get lost in.
    Out there it's frozen,
    footsteps running bank to bank.
Have you friends at home who would like to visit
    The river's hard. Opaque.
    He can't see his face in it.
    It is a hard river.
Can you guess how many visitors we get each year?
It's hard.
Do you know what number you are?

Green

To see herself
        she looks to strangers. The picture
she offers is meant to be beautiful
of a girl, maybe six, in a yellow dress
          on the barge to Tortuguero,
   is a gift I can't refuse.
Brief micas that are her eyes
blink in a settled continent.
        Her old mother's fingers murmur like fish gills
   in her direction—
              be <u>always</u> <u>here</u>.
Whose one breath are they?

But isn't it fine to be one drift in the sinuous
                  contained by a solid green?
In the body of the goose that laid golden egg after egg
In the bottomless cup swilled beyond satiation
   The idea of green expands to keep us afloat.
The idea neither diminishes nor grows.

Possibly the girl is thinking
            destination,
    that far-off look
that makes of her mother a sacked nun
that place where green turtles burrow eggs
   then slip back to the ocean.

How do their thousand hatchlings know the way up
    out of the scratchy heat?
    Out of the holes keep hatching thrashing
slump runners.

How do they know to breathe?
That the spiked air will eat them
is destination?

What parts are interchangeable?
     Where I live, where
                I want to live, transplanted
trillium, white, deepen
violet with age.
            Each dies
to its own color.

Floating Mangers

. . . And so rehung as floating mangers . . .

Thank god (if there was one then) I'm not

one of these ho-hum river boats not Christmas-enough.

.   .   .

And he is standing behind her looking out on the river beyond the table,

explaining tongue-n-groove.

Doggedly around the topic they—

He says something about tomorrow,

he says why-not-take-off-your-coat.

Much of the blood has drained from her knees.

The masts are just ghosts.

Nothing comes off quite easily.

The masts are dipsticks,— any thing to plumb that mud.

Redefinition is a kind of prayer the night convinces and convinces.

(That she wants her coat off, anyway, she doubts.)

[He wanted a room to lock himself in.
    He got the hall.
The line he drew she could not cross.
She scuffed the line, slowly so he could see,
faster than he could catch.
Now he won't tell//   Ask him something   (personal).]

[It locks its claws in the curtain above the patient cat.
It snags; the curtain
snags itself a plush blue knot.
It got the bird. The cat walks.]

The corners of his mouth are gummy.

All of his body

she has narrowed into the thin muscle under his

    Cat-got-your-<u>tongue</u>?!

The shape the words make but not the words,

Not the words and not the lights and then his voice and voices

Around the table running over her — how indifferent strange — their

Tongues are humming are motors running in the almost

Purple air, but what?

What she can't hear above the cats.

Is the lie made more true
        by denying and denying it?
Is truth made a lie
        by mention?
What is the *coat* she needs (what
        is the lie?)
The coat she puts on to take off.

Floating a round in the shape of nervous in the shape of fear,

The boats: Two mangers   A sky of yellow stars   Lights blinking

                                                    HOLY HOLY HOLY;

dawn darkens the lights, slowly

until   HOLY   HOLY   and its essential ghost appear

to claim one another as lovers

one of them drowning   (she is not sure which),

hauling the other with

        its other down.

.   .   .

To put on, to take off

——abrupt as a blood-wound staunched with rag: *Called Back*

With rag, but staunched.

A Convoluted Red Wad of Concentric Circles
Stuck on an Attenuated Column
and Having an Aroma, to My Wife

> *How should one interpret Dr. P.'s peculiar inability to interpret,*
> *to judge, a glove as a glove? . . . A judgment is intuitive, personal,*
> *comprehensive, and concrete—we "see" how things stand, in relation*
> *to one another and oneself. . . . We need the concrete and the real.*
>
> The Man Who Mistook His Wife for a Hat, Oliver Sacks

And do the words ease
in what's real?
Or do words erase the body so the body

won't feel?

Or does description precede their pain
so the pain can be had twice?

I recognize the light but not my wife.
(I wish the sun broke some other way.)
For her body is a hatrack. I touch

her head, feeling

for what to grasp (for what is left
to fall into when my knowing is only

inch by inch?), to shelter me, a wife.

(May comfort borrow her.)

That elm makes form out of the weather.

Old-tree-with-a-hole—

                    (some thing   residential)
I wish the sun——
(I know every name for every thing I've lost.)

How I wish I had a name for what I've lost.

—what can *it* know
of distortion except in brief

puddles, as in
reflection?

I have no
I have to get out now
Thanks for the rid

In Concert

I've left more than one

famous pianist holding his note
while I wondered

peering into the dim auditorium how long
the note would hold after I stopped hearing it.

I feel the soft noose of their listening.
My fingers are dry, the pages stick.

Once I turned two.
The music leapt.

The earthworm cut grows
new bodies, each complete. Not me.

That night a man rapped my hands who
by his next breath made ivory breathe.

Audible, then not. The notes rebound
(some *uni*verse), fireflies

in a dirty jar. I want
sharper edges, the heart-

line pulsing, suddenly flat.
Eternity's bitter, nothing

to snag, to say
here's where it all began.

But what I hold
matches exactly

what they hear: Behold
these notes

half-blackened, now filled in.

Weather

Mt. Hood, May 1986

In another weather
Into the shape of their snow cave.
What few. What survived
The early expedition now stiffens.
Each confirms each other's   Oh,
But the snow was hardly blue and
Up out-of-the-question.

How far down did you go?
                I answered that
postcard-flat against the storm, the four
brown ponies twisted their necks to take in,
perhaps, me, slogging the knee-deep pasture
snow. That's all.
            I was the largest thing
moving anywhere near to look at, buoyant,
like something afloat in—

      (To keep above the avalanche you have to act

                                 as if you are *already*

buried.) You have to fake it. How lost
those others got. The aluminum pole plunged,
probing the snow for something hard
enough to stop it. I have to stop thinking
of the damage to a body a pole could do.
The Trappistines are just up that hill.
If I resort to prayer-in-a-snowstorm it won't last
the next warming trend, I swear; there are blue-

bronze shadows, too, in the holes where the ponies
stand. O

hell, we had the usual discussion—   Is it
harder to live without It, or . . .
Forget it. It doesn't wash. Up there,
whose voices entered me like splinters off
ancestral wood, sing behind the right angle
of the chapel where they can't be seen.
Time will ease them out I know
I know but what
did all that probing
yield but
things to be reburied

Blue Paint Causes Stains in Laboratory Rats

and for that reason, the experiment
continued in another color; Oh

well, even chemical rainbows invent
new ways of having themselves looked at.

We look now new ways at one another:
down, as if we have only wild

mushrooms in mind. And old ways, through weather.
But each time steam swells

into the shape of that inexact
mushroom (unnerved we walk

      under
the new weather
        our mouths open our mouths unfamiliar),

      2
who is the one laughing?

Then we ran out of corridor to walk down and stopped talking.

      In the meantime every night the bodies
of the dead birds are
      they simply reclaimed?

(where is there appetite enough?)

out of our nature—
out of a need to stay—   No, say
I was not here
and though reversals aren't probable
exactly at that
moment the sky, too   oh   fell out
of the bird

Acknowledgments

Grateful acknowledgment is made to the editors of the following periodicals in which some poems in this collection first appeared: *American Letters & Commentary, College English, Colorado Review, Delmar, Denver Quarterly, Field, The Georgia Review, Ironwood, ONTHEBUS, Pavement, Ploughshares, Poetry Northwest,* and *Sonora Review,* and to the editors of the *Anthology of Magazine Verse and Yearbook of American Poetry, 1995–96* and *Outsiders,* in which poems are forthcoming.

Grateful and affectionate acknowledgment to Judith Karolyi and Zenka Bartek of the Karolyi Foundation, and to Hedgebrook, for gifts of time that made writing possible.

Thanks to James Michener and the University of Iowa Writers' Workshop for the generous Paul Engle Fellowship, which helped me complete this book.

And especially to Marvin Bell, James Galvin, and Jorie Graham for their critical encouragement.

To Claudia Bischoff, Michael Frank, Ursula Irwin, Laura Mullen, Robin Reagler, and the MLC Regulars for that and other things.

To my family for everything else.

For the two who are on their way, too.